MYRIAD MANIFESTATIONS OF THE MIND!

TANVI

Dedicated to my

"Parents" and "Teachers"

Contents

Foreword xi

Acknowledgements xiii

1. Leaf 1

2. Expectatation 2

3. The Charisma Of The Sun 3

4. Violin 4

5. Dear Rain 5

6. Beyond 6

7. Love 7

8. The Key Of The World 8

9. The Trees' Request To All Violent 9

10. Understanding 11

11. The Lunatic World 12

12. An Unknown Girl 13

13. Cradle 14

14. Mystrey 15

15. We 16

16. Miss 17

17. Moon 18

18. Pride 19

19. Alone 20

20. City Of Joy 21

21. Someone 22

22. The Rejoice Of Returning At Home 23

Contents

23. Sun	25
24. Happiness & Sadness	26
25. Hill	27
26. Nature	28
27. Self-centered Word	29
28. Stigma	30
29. Exposure	31
30. A Mysterious Answer	32
31. Hope	33
32. Instinct	34
33. Confidence	35
34. Inspire	36
35. Distance	37
36. Sky	39
37. Never	40
38. Gape	41
39. Remember	42
40. Many More	44
41. Again	45
42. Bird	46
43. Loss	47
44. Genuine	48
45. Colour	50
46. Near & Dear	51

Contents

47. Unexpected 52

48. Desire 53

49. Competition 54

50. Equilibrium 55

51. A Sarcastic Reply 56

52. Motherhood 58

53. Harm! 59

54. Social Media 60

55. Perplexing 61

56. Bless Me! 62

57. Her Diverse Role In The Society 63

58. Dismillar 64

59. Incomplete 65

60. Fixed 66

61. Envelope 67

62. Several Formation Of The Mother 68

63. Missunderstanbding 70

64. Dustboin 71

65. Flame Of A Candle 72

Short Story

66. My Dear Inspiration 75

67. Adversary 76

68. Dear Dictionary 77

69. Late 78

Contents

70. Cage — 79

71. Drama — 80

72. Don't Despeir — 81

73. Night Of Weeping — 82

74. My Queen Banana Leaf — 83

75. Dear Mom — 85

76. Change — 86

77. Barrier — 87

78. Dear Internet — 88

79. Music — 89

80. Mind — 90

81. Almighty! — 91

82. Limitless — 92

83. The Conversation Between A Mother Flower And A Baby Flower — 93

84. Chapter — 95

85. Covid-19 — 96

86. My Surprise Birthday Gift — 97

87. A Triangle Love Story Of Sky, Rain & Cloud — 99

88. Motivatition — 100

89. Horror — 101

90. Alone In The City — 103

91. My Room — 104

92. An Adorable Sparrow — 106

Contents

93. Dear — 107

94. Lockdown — 108

95. Help — 109

96. Letters — 110

97. Eloquent — 111

98. Joy! — 112

99. Positive — 113

100. Revenge — 114

101. Examinatition — 115

102. A Simple Mis- Understanding — 116

103. The Days Left Behind — 118

104. The Gift Of The Rain — 120

105. Reality — 122

106. The Diplomacy Of The Nature — 123

107. The Home Of The Clouds — 124

QUOTATIONS — 125

Foreword

In this book, *Myriad Manifestations of the Mind* by **TANVI**, a soul is set up on a treasure hunt to discover herself following the eternal quest of soul perennially entices us.

The mind's expression is embedded in varied forms, from poetry to short stories; they can not be separated from each other, showing that we express and create ourselves in several avenues when we absorb in exploring the infinite landscape of the mind.

I wish you all the success in your new book.

Professor Asim K. Duttaroy
Faculty of Medicine
University of Oslo
Norway

Oslo, June 8, 2021

http://www.asimduttaroy.com

Acknowledgements

I owe much gratitude to My Mother, **Mrs. Neha Naskar**, My Father, **Dr Nurmohammad Naskar PhD**, and My Elder Brother, **Rubaid Naskar**.

I am grateful to my all Respected Teachers, who always encouraged and motivated me to sing, draw, and write.

I am fascinated with Honorable Prof **Asim K Dutta Roy**, *University of Oslo*, who is very fond of *Bengali Literature* and adores the Nobel Laureate poet *Rabindra Nath Tagore* in his all thinking and research. He has given me a foreword for my book **"Myriad Manifestations of the Mind,"** which provides me boundless joy. I have a deep sense of gratitude for him, who has read my poetries, quotations, and short stories.

Last but not the least, my heartfelt thanks to my other Brother, Soumik Saha, for reading and analyzing every item of the book with lots of love.

An exceptional thanks to our close associate **Mr. Sayan Banik** for publishing & editing this book and provides me a big platform to reach the readers. Few words are not sufficient to describe my parents for their enthusiasm towards my all endeavors.

1

If I were a falling leaf
I knew it from earlier that,
My place will be under the Feet of the people.
In spite of, I never got disappointed.
Because, it was expected, the people,
Who are so much "Rich" one,
Who "Diminish" each and everything
as well as each and everyone,
I might be nothing to them.
But, the people,
Who are so much Distressed & Underprivileged,
Who don't even have any shoes under their soles,
They would treat me like "God"
I would be the Soft Sponge to them.
So, I wouldn't have any "Regrets" in my life.

2

Expectatation

My body tells me Please,
Nurture me like a Baby,
Cherish me like a Plant,
Maintain me like Furniture,
Love me like a Mother,
Support me like a Father,
Never ignore me like an unknown person.
Always, try to keep me healthy like Butter,
Try to help me to get sunshine for Vitamin D
Do you know?? Why am I telling you all these??
I am telling all these only for your betterment
because the body is yours.
And, if your body is fit and fine,
Your mental health will be cultivated.

3

THE CHARISMA OF THE SUN

Today's sunshine is totally different than the other day.
It's literally shimmering like the "Glass of Mirror".
In which, I could even see my own "Reflection".
And the most Fascinating thing is,
When it was falling on the leaves of the Tree,
It looks as if someone has scattered the "Golden Stars"
Can you just imagine "The Glory of the Sun"?

4

VIOLIN

In the Midnight,
A "Mystical Sound" snatched my sleep.
All of a sudden, I sat up with a thud.
I could see somebody behind the curtain playing on
Instrument.
Aahhaa! What a Wiz Music filled my mind,
I tremendously forced to follow his "Reflexion"
as far as he went.
He truly made me wacky.
After that, slowly slowly the Shadow disappeared.
But, why did he entangle me in his "Sorcery"?
However, who was "He"???

5
DEAR RAIN

Have you come at last Maa?
Ohh!! Thanks to the Almighty
But, why are you so late?
Do you know how long days they have been eagerly
waiting for you?
Do you know how long days they haven't eaten
anything??
They are really very hungry.
They are really very thirsty Maa.
I can no longer see their sufferings.
I beg you of Maa, to feed them as per your capability so
that they can get their lives back.
Otherwise they will suffocate in the Black Smoke of this
Violent World
Please, don't disappoint them because they all are truly
very tempted for you "Rain".
Yes!! Just only for you!

6

Beyond

Love is a word of 4 letters.
It's not so easy calculation.
To somebody it's a Game,
To somebody it's an Illusion,
To somebody it's a Fascination,
But what is the actual answer?
Even if our lives are over, we will not be able to
Understand the "Real Meaning" the "Real Using"
& the "Real Significance" of this 4 letters.

7

Love

Love doesn't have,
Any specific time
Any specific date
Any specific age
Any specific season
Any specific place
Anyone, Anytime and Anywhere
One person can fall in love with another person.

8

THE KEY OF THE WORLD

The Door of the World has totally been closed
for a long time.
I can't find out the Key by no means.
Even I don't remember where I have kept it.
I have searched for Thousand Times.
Yet, I didn't rescue it.
Then, The KEY was not stolen??
Oh my God.
If so, please somebody help me to get it out.
I would like to go to my Mother
Because I am Out of Breath.
Please can someone open the "Door"??

9

THE TREES' REQUEST TO ALL VIOLENT

If trees could talk, they would have said,
We also feel pain while PEOPLE hurt us,
We also feel cry While PEOPLE misbehave with us,
We have also blood like the "HUMANS",
We have also emotions like the "HUMANS",
We have also lives like the "HUMANS",
We have everything like the "HUMANS",
But the one major issue is that,
We just can't talk like the "HUMANS",
This is why everybody tortures on us.
But, we promise, if you get rid of us,
One day we will make this "UNIVERSE"
SACRED GLAMOROUS
One day we will make this "UNIVERSE"
with so much "Magics" that
You people don't have to take breath artificially.
Hence, thinking about the future of "ALL"...
We are folding our hands to you
Don't cut us,

Please don't cut us.
Otherwise, Your living place will destroy very shortly.

10

10

Understanding

It's not my fault
Because the people,
Whom I believed very shortly,
Whom I loved without doubting,
Whom I gave shelter in the corner of my mind,
Lastly, they cheated on me. They used me like a
Agni Gel Pen which is famous as
Use and Through. So, in that case, conversely,
I have received a lot of Virtues from the God.

11

THE LUNATIC WORLD

What a day we have brought at last!!
We have totally changed our World clock.
Moreover, we have changed our Nature Mother as well.
How could we do that??
We should be ashamed of ourselves.
Because, those birds, who are supposed
to chirping in the morning,
They are roaming around and whispering at night only
for
our carelessness???
Oops! What we have done.
As much as quantity of poison we have spread
everywhere,
our World has become insane at last.
We are "Unforgivable" to God.

12

AN UNKNOWN GIRL

I have been noticing you for so long time.
In the same way, you have been staring at the
"Wave of the Sea."
Even you didn't blink of your eyes for once.
By any chance are you waiting for the waves coming to
you?
If I guess, I am right...
Then, according to my counsel,
They will never come to you for holding your hands
Dear.
So don't wait anymore.
Go back to your destiny.

13

Cradle

Parents are "The Presentment of God" to me.
The safety shelter like Beneath the Tree.
The place of love like the left side of heart.
The place of anger like the Fire of Sun.
The place of happiness like the open sky.
The place of worship like the mosque or church and the
place of each and everything in which I will never feel
any
insecurity for sure by closing my eyes as long as I will
live.

14

Mystrey

Today, the moon is smiling sarcastically,
Because, the whole world seems to be dark in this little
cloudy weather.
There are no stars in the sky.
Sometimes, the moon is also playing Hide and Seek
with
the cloud.
But, so what?? Right this moment,
There is no other arrangement of lights in this limitless
sky
without her.
Hence, don't underestimate anyone.
One day everyone will need everyone.

We are Militant on social media.
We are Defendant on social media.
We are Favorable on social media.
We are Sympathetic on social media.
We are Human on social media.
We are Integrated on social media.
Now, the question is that??
Why are we all on social media like that?
The first & foremost answer is to
become Renowned in our
Dramatic Stage of Life like the Reel Life of all the
Actors & Actresses.
Then, what about our real life?
We are totally opposite over there & not one of them.
So, behind this face and mask
Which is the real "We"?

16
miss

Today I am very solitary.
Nobody is there to make me Happy.
Nobody is there to make me Angry.
Nobody is there to make me Cry.
Nobody just Nobody.
Even I know that nobody couldn't be there.
But still, why doesn't the mind want to accept that??

17

Moon

The moon is asleep
Don't shout
Let her take rest
She is so much tired of giving her golden light to shine
our
universe all the time.

18
Pride

Vanity???
Hahahahaha
No No No Dear
I don't have it.
Even I didn't have it earlier.
And I won't have it ever.
But the people don't want to make it out at all
Always, they judge me from their own perspectives.
But never from my side!!!
So what??
I just don't care all those rubbish people.

19

Alone

Being alone at home feel like,
An "Orphan Child".
And that moment,
I can experience more and more
The Value of Absence of
The Key of Hope in my life.
Hence, in this entire world, I think so,
Nothing can be more "Unfortunate"
than become an Orphan.

20

City of Joy

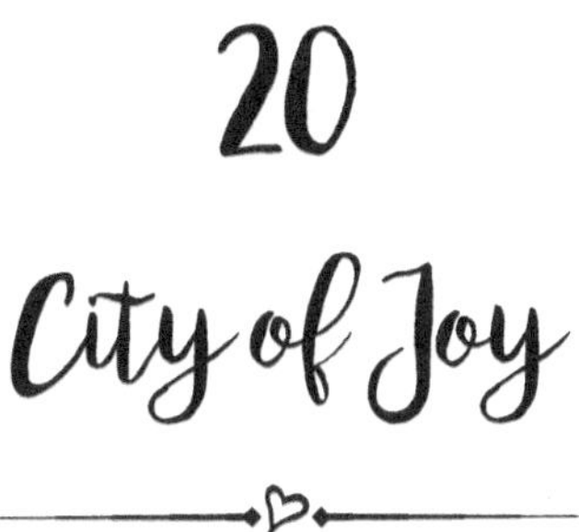

One day, I just want to visit Kolkata
"The City of Joy" at night with my
Elder brother in which,
There will be no noise, There will be no mob,
There will be no traffic jams on the road,
Only, there will be a little raining at Ganges Ghat and I can
take breath with Open Soul..

21
SOMEONE

I was in more pain while I saw him.
One time,
I had a lot of fight with him,
I had a lot of chit-chat with him,
I had a lot of conversation with him,
Even, I travelled a lot with him everywhere.
But like,
The lightening without clouds
Everything has totally become changed.
Today,
He is cool like the Statue.
And his eyes are tranquil like the river.
However, why is it so?
Then,
Is this called the Changeable Chapter of Life???

22

THE REJOICE OF RETURNING AT HOME

It's been about One Year
I am so so far from my Paradise.
Today, no how, I couldn't concentrate on my studies.
Even, I opened not a single page of my book.
Actually, as the establishment is too much monumental
in our lives,
So we are bound to sacrifice something to get
something better
Yet despite all those, end of the day, we all are the
people
of flesh and blood.
I was shaded the whole day.
So, in the dusk, I went to the terrace and looked at the
sky.
A flock of birds were returning to their destination
talking

to each other,
After finishing their task which suddenly increased
my suppressed
Anguish a lot that can't be expressed by words.
Yes!! I obviously understand really,
There is a different delight to return at home,
Isn't it???
But, my hands and feet are tied with chain.

23

Sun

You look so beautiful like the egg yolk
You look so sweet like the orange
Your cymbals is like the golden ray
Everything about you is so much appreciative
Even we know, without you the whole world will
undergo
into dark.
But why are doing like that Sun?
Why are you so much angry nowadays??
We know that, we are the destroyer.
But, who are innocent, like -
The birds can't fly beside you getting scared.
The trees are feeling like fatal.
Moreover, we the felonious are almost feeling deadly
only
because of our acridity.
Yet, I earnestly request you don't be furious so much.
Please, don't kill us Sun.
Please, don't kill us.
I bet to you our lives.

24

HAPPINESS & SADNESS

What do you think about them?
Happiness & Sadness.
They both are friends of each other?
No dear. You are totally wrong.
Rather, they both are enemies of each other.
Always, a strong fight goes on between them,
Who will take place in the people's mind?
But for having a lot of ominous power,
The devil might temporarily win the game and for
being so sensitive,
The angel gets defeated most of the time.
But never forget dear,
The truth & honesty will always prevail forever.

25

Will

You are really very mysterious.
How did you enchant me?
You know what?
Always, I can hear your calling.
Always, I can feel you deeply.
Even, Always, I get a holy smell from your body.
Will you please tell me?
Which fragrance do you use?
Because, I literally fell in love with you.
Will you be mine forever??

26

Nature

Today, while I was sitting beside the window
and was fully
engrossed to take the fragrance of the nature,
The stormy wind,
The lightening flashes,
The thunderstorm,
The drizzle,
The drop of water on the green wet leaf,
The sweet rhythmic sound of the falling rain in the
pond,
Most importantly, the smell of the wet soil,
All these precious gifts from the nature really brought
tears
to my eyes unknowingly.
But I don't know why?
May be, I ever had a deep connection with my mother
(nature).
If, there is any connection at all earlier,
So, I am blessed in a word.

27

Self-Centered Word

I lived in peace until
I didn't learn to understand the definition of this Self-Centered world.
I didn't learn to understand the definition
of this harsh reality.
And, at last, I didn't learn to understand the
definition of the masked people.
Opps!!! My goodness!!!
Now, I feel, I was the happiest person in that time.

28
STIGMA

Whenever, thousands and thousands girls are being
raped by thousands and thousands ferocious beasts,
each and every day.
Those raped girls are just unacceptable, outcast
untouchable, slut, in a word. And most importantly, the
venomous word which impacts more and more on
those
victims by our so-called society is stigmatized.
But, never forget one thing,
The moon has also the stigma on her body.
Is she outcast?
Is she unacceptable?
Is she untouchable?
Is she slut?
Rather, on the contrary,
She is the elegance of this universe.

29

Exposure

To enlighten in the "Light of Education"
To enlighten in the "Light of Behaviour"
To enlighten in the "Light of Conscience"
into those people who are still living in
the dark forest of their lives.
Only and only, especially for them, I want
to be the "Light of the Lamp"

30

A MYSTERIOUS ANSWER

Today...
Am "I" Tired? Or is my "Mind" tired?
Trust me, I don't know the exact answer.
And, that's why I have been trying to mitigate it for so
long
time.
But no. I became failure over again and again.
Well?? Somehow,
Isn't my "Mind" trying to make me tired??
Can anyone please tell me??
What is the reason behind this "Tiredness"???

31

Hope

Life Greets me
When I never give up, despite lots of
Obstacles in front of me,
When I never get tired by fighting continuously with
lots
of difficulties,
When I have the success, overcoming all the hardships,
My life never demotivates me. It waits me to become a
victorious and to see a big smile on my face.
My life is a book of inspiration for me.

32

34

Instinct

—♡—

For me writing is like,
An addiction like the mango juice in the summer
season,
An emotion like the deep black cloud in the rainy
season,
A loneliness partner like the sweet sunshine in the
winter
afternoon,
A fallen leaf and the breeze in the spring season.
In a word, writing is a part of my nature mother.

33

Confidence

I am hiding from those people
Who are ambidextrous like snake
Who are violent like lion
Who are howling like tiger
Who are fake like mask
But, would you like to know why?
Because, being associated with those frauds,
I don't want to finish my life from the shining light of
this
glamorous world.

34

Inspire

Life speaks to me,
When, I feel low or demotivate,
being confined at home like a prisoner.
When, I don't get any motivation,
any inspiration to do any work.
When, I can't concentrate on my study,
When, I feel hopeless,
When, I get scared thinking about
this present destructing situation.
But despite all those, life tells me one important thing
which is about patience and mental strength that is the
topmost medicine for this disaster.

35
DISTANCE

You know what? You are so much furious that
everybody gets afraid of you.
You know what? You are so much outrageous
that everybody hates you.
You know what? How many people have bleeding
arrows
in their heart every day?
You know what? How many people cry so loudly every
day?
Can you see that bleeding of those hearts?
Can you hear that sounds of their crying?
No you can't. Because, you don't have any impetus.
You are so much
Hoggish, that only you know,
how to separate everyone from each other.
More often I think,
you have a big problem in your life & i.e. you never feel
happy about yourself and don't want anyone to be
happy.
That's why, nobody loves you and you will never be able
to

make a satisfactory place in the corner of the people's
mind.
Just one thing, I would like to tell you,
I hate you distance.
I just hate you.

36
Sky

Today, since the morning, His mood is not good.
He is looking very gloomy.
His face seems to be black like ink.
How many times, I have asked, what happened? At least share with me.
But, by no means, he is saying nothing. Such a repressed boy!!
Now, see his crying like a baby. Oops, what a mess!!
Just one simple thing, he doesn't want to understand, If he suppresses his pain, his trouble in his mind, None will suffer more than him.
So get a little annoyed,
I asked him not a single question further and thought,
Let him cry as much as he can,
If the mind is little lighter??

37

Never

The bucket list of funny things in life are: To think yourself
very clever or cunning, To think yourself very wisdom.
To criticize others. To mock others.
To copy others.
To trust others within a very short time. But what
happened at last?

38

Gape

Where were you for so long days?? Why didn't you come?
Do you know??
Every day, I sat down and waited for you like a Pilgrim
Crow.
Every day, I thought, you might come now. But,
No. You didn't come.
Every day you disappointed me. I am really very angry
with you. I don't want to talk to you.
Acha??
Were you not in any danger??
Were you not captivated to someone?? Oh my
goodness!! If it's so,
Then, you have suffered a lot. I apologize to you.
Because, I have said a lot just without listening
anything. But, I might guess,
Who they can be!! I think,
They are none other than the "Felon Cloud & Rain"
Anyway,
Don't worry my beloved sunlight Just, don't worry at all.
I will see them.

39

Remember

———❦———

Even, today, whenever, I remember her, I feel so week.
I feel so lonely.
I feel like running her immediately.
In spite of, I never let anyone understood. Always, I
behaved very normally with everyone. Actually,
The memories are very powerful. They don't want to
move so easily.
They don't let to forget anything so effortlessly. Okay.
No problem.
I have to fight with them as per my capabilities. I don't
want to keep any relationship with those, Who didn't
respect my parents?
Who didn't give any value of them who loved her
unconditionally?
Most importantly.
Who didn't give any worth of my education, whom I
literally worship.
Always, who led her life so roughly doing lots of late
night parties, clubs & all.
And, that's why,
I have no longer communication with her today. But,

I thought her as my own sister. Yes! The sister of my own blood. Then, why did she betray with me? May be, This is called the Destiny of Life.

43

40

Many More

♡

Accha??
Can't we have any desires, any hopes, any dreams like
the rich one?
Definitely, we can have. That's why, like all.
A lot of wills,
A lot of expectations, A lot of fancy,
We showcase in our mind.
And, do a lot of hard works also to fulfill each and every
Above Word.
But, what's the benefit to keep it all ??? What's the
benefit??
When, despite having all these, sometimes,
We are compelled to destroy each letter of each word in
front of our eyes,
with a heavy stone pressed to the chest and a big smile
on our face by the Hammer??
Actually, you know?? We should not have any Big
Imagination
Because, we are middle class people. Yes!! We are!!!

41

Again

I always wanted to write about all those,
I always wanted to implement about all those I always
wanted to express about all those, Even,
You don't have any idea
How many times I tried to do that!! But, I noticed a
thing,
As many times as I went to jot down, My "Pen" trembled
again and again. My "Pen" stopped me again and again. My
"Pen" never cooperated with me. So, eventually,
I became collapse. Yes, I became.
Actually, might be,
They never wanted to be disclosed to the public. Well ?
For so long time, I said so much, but, nobody asked me for
once.
Who are they?
Okay, then, I am revealing it now. They are one & only
My lost memories,
Who are intimately involved in each of my veins of the
body.

42

Bird

Today,
A cockatoo bird was sitting on the stand of the cradle
on my rooftop.
Seeing her, I was going to touch her with lot of
affections. But, before my arrival, she flew away.
That made me heartbroken.
Hmm, that made me heartbroken, may be, for few
hours. Still, thereafter, I realised,
Even a bird also knows that,
"The Human Beings are Executioner."

43

Loss

Sometimes
I love to jailbird some feelings in the Hutch of my mind.
Rather, once in a while, I realise, It would be better to
keep those Sentiments in my Heart.
Yes!! It would be better. That might not be revealed??
What's the loss in it??

44

Genuine

Yes it's 100 % true that, The whole day I scold you, The
whole day I shout on you,
The whole day I get angry with you, The whole day I
argue with you, Even,
The whole day I dominate you,
And, for all these, I might be very Rough & Tough to
everyone.
Acha???
Did they ever try to understand?
How much "Love & Care" is hidden in everything??
Yeah, today, I confess myself,
I might can't speak softly,
I might can't behave politely, But,
That doesn't mean,
I am too much arrogant.
It's all of my outside pictures. Actually, like others,
I couldn't express every my love, care & all.
That's why, nobody couldn't see my inside & I don't
want to show that at all.
Hence, I request to you cordially, Never mind for my
haughtiness Because, end of the day,

I am just a piece of paper without you 'DAD'.

49

45

Colour

You don't even know yourself How are you looking today!!
A Deep "Red Saree" with Golden edge, A Deep "Red
Blouse" with Golden edge, A little "Red Tip" on forehead,
A little "Golden Nosepin",
A "Golden Long Chain" in neck, A "Golden Bangle" in
hand,
A "Golden Finger ring" & Long Earrings", Along with,
Open "Black Curly Hair", And, Lastly,
A Sweet Smile on face.
Oh my God!! I am totally impressed. I just can't take my
"Eyes" off you.
Will you please sit by my head all night and put me to
sleep??
Because, today, it really seems like,
A "Red Fairy" has come down from the "Olympus" with
her "Unparalled Beauty"
"My Beloved Mom."

46

Near & Dear

I never thought earlier, One day,
I have to face this.
Today one of my near & dear one came to the door of
my house,
But, I couldn't tell him to come inside. I just saw him
from so far,
But, I couldn't touch him, He was so much thirsty,
But, I couldn't give him a glass of water.
I felt guilty too much from my inside that the whole
day, I can't forgive myself.
Even, I feel like killing myself. Oh, God! Lastly,
What type of cruel day we have brought!!!

47

Unexpected

Today
There is a strong thunderstorm at a speed of about 185
kms. Oh shit!!
All the trees are swaying so loudly, It seems, as if,
The merry-go-round is spinning. Then, what about all
the birds??
They are too much helpless right this moment.
Even, they are not being able to understand, where they
should go??
Because, nowhere, they are safe.
Neither in the sky nor in the branches of trees. In spite
of understanding everything,
I am impotent too like them.
If I want, I can't stop this insanity. Oh ! God please save
them.
Otherwise, they will die. Because they don't have any
Veiled-home like us.

48

Desire

I want to sleep. Trust me.
I really want to sleep. Even, you know?
Before sleep,
Neither I get engaged on social media by using mobile
phone nor with laptop and so on.
Yet, I can't.
No.
I just can't by trying for Two Thousand times, But, one
thing,
I tend to think,
Isn't there any deep conspiracy is going on behind me??
Hmmm.
That might be!!
Because, for so long months, I am getting a different
kind of smell.

49

Competition

Today
All the infants of our world mother are maddened with
the game of loosing and winning.
Because, our mother is too much sick right this
moment. She has become completely silent like a dumb
person,
As after a heavy shower as the nature becomes calm
down. That's why, by hook or by crook,
Being the babies of the mother,
It's our superior responsibility to make her healthy as
early as possible.
Otherwise, there might have the flag of victory in
someone's hand,
And
There might have the stone of tomb in someone's hand.

50
Equilibrium

Trying so hard to adjust with the situation, Trying so hard
to be normal with everyone, Trying so hard to be
accustomed with everything, But, no
I can't do one of them. Seriously,
I can't anymore. Now,
I am just mentally disturbed.
This harsh circumstance has sucked my all energies
and all positivity.
Oh, my lord!!
Will you please give me more strength for fighting this
tenacious war??
Because, I am totally fatigued, Trust me,
I am totally fatigued.

51

A SARCASTIC REPLY

You know what??
Today, I have got some messages from someone!! Yes!! I have got.
And, it's definitely my pleasure that, they give me more importance,
They give me more priority.
Even, they have some time to think about me!! Oh my God!!
I am really very lucky, But you tell me,
What are you thinking??
By any chance, aren't you thinking, I have got any love proposal?
No No No.
My sweetheart, You are false,
But it's terrible true that I have got something, But, that all are slangs messages,
That all are pornography.
Uff!! I am just getting tired of laughing. Anyway, who cares???

I am honored that my efficiency could make them
malicious.

57

52

MOTHERHOOD

He is addicted to heroin He is addicted to alcohol He is addicted to smoking
He comes back at home after 2 AM at late night. Or, someday, he doesn't come back at home.
Nobody knows, where does he spend the night? Nobody knows, with whom he spends the night? Nobody knows, what does he do at night.
As,
All types of heinous work he has done,
To the book of society, he is already known as a criminal. To the book of his father, he is known as an abandoned. Then? What about the book of his mother??
Listen!!
To the book of his mother - he is always known as auspicious.
And, this is the, Superiority of motherhood
No matter how worst the child is, She can never discard them.

53

Dear Smokers,
I just want to say something to you all and i.e. You
smoke.
Okay,
You smoke as much as you wish.
Nobody will stop you because it's totally your personal
matter.
But, fulfilling your own desires, Why are you harming
others lives?

54
Social Media

Nowadays, the whole day, As, on one side,
We are chatting on WhatsApp, Messenger, Instagram
and all.
Again, on the other side,
We are equally chatting with our mind. How much
foregoing we are!!
Isn't it?
But, it has to admit that, Seriously,
it's too much difficult to handle both of them together.

55

Perplexing

Today
My mind is very cloudy.
Just like a cloudy sky. As if, so dark around me.
Not even wanting to do anything since morning. And,
As well as headaches.
Uff!! What an excruciating pain. I really can't tolerate
anymore. But,
Why the day is so awkward??

56

Bless me!

———❤———

May be, I saw you.
May be, I never saw you again. I can't remember at all.
I heard later from my parents,
You had given me a Name, what affects me till date.
Only, your face, what I saw in the album, float into my eyes always.
I never had that Good Fortune To interact with you.
To listen to the stories from you, like other,
"Grandfathers & Granddaughters." Because,
You left me long years back.
I saw your frozen body that I remember. But, I was so little that time.
I didn't understand the meaning of your last day. I didn't understand.
Today you are no more. You are nowhere.
So, what?
You will always be in my memories. Bless me.

57

Her diverse role in the society

She is introvert. She is voiceless. She is peaceful.
Again, the same person is Arrogant.
Snooty. Impolite.
And, much more!!! Oh my god!!
Does it happen at all?
Isn't it so much astonishing? Yes,
But in spite of all those,
She is really very thankful to God. To provide her so
many qualities. To make her more appreciations.
Because, she has got a very beautiful name: "Versatile
Girl".

58

Dismillar

Dear Summer, Do you know?
You are just like the Five Fingers of the hand. Either
favourable or objectionable.
Either comfortable or onerous. Either thriller or
terrible.
But. Don't get upset. It's not your fault.
Actually,
The position of each and
every human being in this earth is isolated. And,
You have to accept it.

59

Incomplete

Dear Laziness, I know,
You don't like me a little bit.
Even, not only you but also, a lot of people. But,
I don't think for once, why I am so much irritating to
you. Rather,
I always try to abolish the difficulties from my life as
much as I can.
If, I give them the chance to enter at one time, they will
keep misusing it.
And, I never want to slaughter my life with my own
hand. So, get lost and stay away from me.
Never try to contact me in my entire life. I won't let you
in by any means.

60
Fixed

He has no specific Language. He has no specific Status.
He has no specific Gender. He has no specific Color. He
has no specific Caste. He has no specific Religion.
He has no specific Race, Even, He has no specific Dress.
He is "SECULAR" like our Secular Country. He is
"EQUAL" for all in this Universe.
But....
He is the Heroic and Bloodcurdling Person,
Who can demolish the "Audacity" of all in a second.
Who can abolish the "Differentiation" of all in a second.
Who can transform the Smile into Crying in an instant.
Who can be understood only & only through the " Facial
Expressions".
Do you know? Who is He? Very much confusing.......
Isn't it??
Actually, He is very down to earth, none other than
our......
"PAIN"

61

ENVELOPE

Nobody gives you Priority. Nobody loves you at all.
Rather, everybody uses you only for their purposes.
They don't know, how much beneficial you are!!
They don't know, you have a variety of roles. You are a
"Messenger".
You are a "Social Worker".
You carry out the news of Happiness. You carry out the
news of Sadness.
And, even without you,
Nothing will reach to the correct person. And, even,
without you,
All are "Invaluable". All are "Irrelevant". All are
"Inconsistent".
But, inspite of all those,
Why don't the people understand your "Importance"??

62

SEVERAL FORMATION OF THE MOTHER

What a power of the Sky!!
Only for its Blue Color, sometimes the surroundings are
turned into Blue just like the Blue Water of the Sea.
What a power of the Sun!!
Due to the Yellow Light of its intense heat, sometimes
all around is turned into Yellow just like the Marigold
Flower. What a power of the Moon !!
Only for it's White Moonlit Light , sometimes all around
is turned into White just like the Fairies.
What a power of the Dark Cloud!!
Only for its Black colour,sometimes the neighbouring is
turned into Black just like the Coal.
And,
What a power of the Stars!!
Only for its Flickering Light, sometimes the adjacent is
turned into Glitter.

Ufff!!! Oh My Goodness!!! Will you please tell me, How many "Forms" will you showcase anymore?

63

Missunderstanbding

Words are very very mischievous. They always try to create
the difference of opinion between the two.
The always try to create the fight between the two. They
always try to create the unrest between the two. They
always try to create the distance between the two. And,
lastly,
They create separation between the two. But, do you
know? What is it called??
It's nothing but the
"Misunderstanding".

64

Dustboin

You are not important to us. We tremendously hate you.
We cover our noses with our hands.
We feel like vomiting while we go beside you. Why?????
Because,
you are dirty. you have odor.
you are one of the most damned places in the world.
But, one thing we forget always and that is
We never realise your significance. We never
understand that,
merely for you all our houses become clean. And that's
why,
You are not at all irrelevant rather your consideration is
beyond all- "DUSTBIN".

65

Flame of a Candle

Suppose, right now, there are no lights. Then, what will happen??
People will get scared. Is it??? Am I right??
Yes....
But I will not get afraid for once at all.
And, for that, there is a mystery behind that. Do you know what???
Okay, Now, listen carefully & silently.....
At first, I will close my eyes and just remind the face of my mother which shall automatically start working as the "Flame of a Candle". Suppose, right now, there are no lights. Then, what will happen?? People will get scared.
Is it??? Am I right?? Yes....
But I will not get afraid for once at all.
And, for that, there is a mystery behind that. Do you know what???
Okay, Now, listen carefully & silently.....
At first, I will close my eyes and just remind the face of my mother which shall automatically start working as the "Flame of a Candle".

Short Story

66

my DEAR INSPIRATION

Hope you are doing well. After so so long time, I am writing this letter to you. Please don't get angry with me. Actually my exam was going on and that's why I couldn't manage my time to talk to you. But you know what?? Always you prevail in my mind at another level that I can't make you understand. You are like a "Tree Bole" to me & without you the meaning of my life will completely be "meaningless". So, my dear inspiration, I earnestly request you to come to home as early as possible. Your coming would be my great pleasure.

67

ADVERSARY

One morning, I sat on my bed beside the window with cross-legged and was reading a book and taking a cup of coffee with a relaxed mood. I was totally absorbed in that ambience. Suddenly, a little sweet bird flew away and started making a knock on my window glasses though it was closed. At least for 10 minutes, the bird was doing that. The funny thing was that, she never got tired for once rather got angry more and more. But, I had not been able to find out any reason behind that what was going on actually over there. I was observing very consciously. But, lastly with a lot of trouble, I discovered that, she thought one of her "RIVAL" was there and she was looking for that. I understood, she couldn't tolerate an opponent on her opposite side. Hence, the point to be noted here, Nobody either human beings or animals, or birds can endure his or her antagonists.

68

DEAR DICTIONARY

You are made up of millions and millions of pages.

You are made up of millions and millions of words.

You are made up of millions and millions of meanings. But, in this era, you see, Nobody gives you the priority.

You are just irrelevant to the new generation.You are just invaluable to the new generation.They don't love you. They don't care for you at all.Because Google has given all the interpretations of their lives.

69

LATE

That day, yet I remember, I had been waiting for you for so long hours at the station. I had been calling you for hundred times. But the phone was ringing and ringing only. You didn't receive the call.

That was a winter night and the time was at around 11.00 PM. Nobody was around me there. Only two or three "Teasers" were talking within themselves and were laughing at me. My whole body got cold like an "Ice" and my hands and legs were shivering.

Thereafter, I noticed two or three pairs of legs were coming towards me. And when I took an attempt to run, suddenly I had a push with someone. But within a lot of dread, I found a peace to see him and that was "You", who were supposed to come at 8 PM. But, still today, some questions arise in my mind, what was the reason behind his coming so late?? But I couldn't ask him ever by watching his ignorable appearance. So, I think, if he was not there that day, I might not be here today. So, let's keep some curiosities in the mind.

70

Cage

Today all the birds are laughing at us.

Do you know why?? Because whenever we keep them in a cage,

They suffer a lot, they tremendously squirm to get rid of this prison.

They become anxious for coming back to their destination. But we people are so much selfish. We don't want anyone to understand.

This is why, the bird species, cursed all the mankind for torturing them ruthlessly.

And now see, what a tragic situation of us!!

We are confined in the cage, we are getting punishment for our crimes and the "Innocuous Birds" are flying in the sky freely.

71

Drama

This world seems to be a platform of competition.

Everyone is busy giving ace to everyone...

And by doing this competition, now, the values, humanity, honesty everything have been lost from the mankind today!!

How much drastic!! Isn't it??

72

Don't Despeir

We should never regret about our height, face, skin- tone and much more because everyone has some limitations in their lives. But embracing all those limitations we have to prove that, we all are perfect and victorious in our own way of living.

73
Night of Weeping

Only the night listen to the sound of my "Sobbing Cry". Because while, he crossed the entry gate with his heavy luggage and passport, there was not a single drop of water in my eyes. I stood like a wooden doll. I stood like a rock and the lump of tears were stuck in my throat. I stared at him as the same way as a tiger targets his hunting.

My eyelids didn't fall even once. My chest was bursting with tears that day. Even, still, every night, I cry silently. But nobody knows about all those. May be, I never wanted to show my feelings, my emotions like others to get some typical sympathy. And, that's why, my "Night of Weeping" will be mine forever.

74

MY QUEEN BANANA LEAF

It had been raining profusely since the dawn and I was supposed to go outside for some important works in the morning.

That's why, watching the grotty situation, I was resentful and sat down impatiently and waiting for the rain to stop. But there is no one who has ever been able to neglect the beauty of nature and this is why, I could not despite a thousands of nagging. My eyes were stuck to notice a sweet thing. My Queen Banana Leaf, beside my window, is looking very glad and glamorous than the other day. She is literally blushing. Her cheeks turned into pinkish colour with shame. But why is it so? I asked her out of curiosity.

Anything Special my darling? Did your prince charming come? And she said with a little smile on her face down: Yes and he just touched me by the colour of his love. Thereafter, I asked her with a great excitement, please tell me, tell me, I am dying to listen to about him, who is he? But I was totally flabbergasted to hear her answer.

She replied: He is none other than my fascinating hero - "Rain".

75

DEAR MOM

You are the embodiment of power for carrying me in your womb for 9 months.

You are the epitome of tolerance by enduring pain equal to mountains for showing me the bright light of this world.

You are as eternal truth as every eternal things in this universe. Your wrath is as bloodshot as the fire of the sun. Your smile is as transparent as the light of the moon.

Your eyes are as quicksilver as the shining stars. Your love is as soft as your lip. Mom, you know what??

You are as coltish as the rain. You are as roaring as the cloud. You are so so expensive that the gold, diamond and even platinum will confess their defeat. You are one of the most secured, hopeful and peaceful places in my life.

So, the golden gift which I have received once by the grace of almighty, will always try to showcase it very carefully. Even, I die before you, I won't have any regret, because I will know, once upon a time, I gained the vicinity like a god-like woman until the last breathe of my life.

Your loving daughter.

76

Change

If I had a time turner, changing this current situation, I would have gone back to my childhood memories which I left behind 20 years back. Today, standing on this terrible situation, now, I could feel that, at that time, everything was so much simple and innocent.

Each and every day was like the shining stars in the sky. Even, each and every little grumpy with my sibling was so much sweet like sugar, each and every little game such as Hide and Seek, Kanamachi with the childhood friends were like the Green Grassess and the Transparent Sky without clouds. In a word, there was no complexity. I think, that was the best part, still, this is the best part and this will be the best part until the last day of my life.

77

Barrier

The whole world seems to be confined in the prison.

A silence is prevailing all around But the mind is always anxious, May be something is missing But what??

I think everyone knows that answer.

78

DEAR INTERNET

For a second without you the whole world feels lonely,

For a second without you the whole mankind feels crazy and anxious

Even for a second without you a little baby feels like a cry, Please tell me one thing...

How did you subdue all of them?? Do you have any mysterious power??

I have to really appreciate your charisma that you have brought the whole world in the palm of everyone's hand.

79

music

The definition of music varies from person to person.

If, on one side, it's worship to someone, so, on the other hand, it's devotion to others.

Again, it's passion or inspiration to someone, so it's entertainment to others.

But, apart from those, did we ever think that it can be something which can keep a person mentally & physically healthy and happy?

Did we ever think that it can be mightier than some prescribed poisonous medicines??

No, we never thought it that way. Actually, we didn't want to think ever.

But, today, standing on this destructing situation, we have to know that music is not only an Art but also a therapy. It is that sword which can evoke a response in a comatose patient and even a straight line can be curved as well by the grace of music. Now, can you imagine its magical power??

80

Mind

Sometimes she is very lively like the golden sunlight, Again, sometimes she is very melancholic like the cloudy sky,

Sometimes she is very saddened like the dead tree, Again, sometimes she is very aloof like the stars. Isn't it really very difficult to understand her?? Yes!! Actually she is variable like the season.

But despite all those variations of her mood, we can't leave her because she is one and only wardrobe in which we keep everything. Do you know? Who is she?

She is none other than our "Mind."

81
Almighty!

God has created this universe with the human beings.

We all are connected with each other. But now see, what a day has come!!

Today a distance has been made between each other. How much astonishing!! Isn't it??

82

Limitless

Today there are enormous stars in the sky.

Our sky also got dressed up with lots of shining and glamorous lights.

Actually, today the Polaris is getting married with her loving person that I got to know from the Phosper in the morning. I could hear the screaming of their merriments,

I could hear that, everybody was wishing them A Very Happy Married Life & Long Years of Togetherness.

And, all those things, I was noticing since the evening.

But, I was looking at the sky in the same way and the tears were falling from my eyes constantly. Even, I know, everyone might feel laughing to hear it, why I am "Dusky and Crying" watching the marriage of the stars.

Actually, the Polaris always used to tell me that, I am his one and only best friend. But I am astonished to think it, why he didn't share this happy news with me for once??

How could he forget me?

So, was there any deficiency in my friendship? Might be...

That's why, from today onwards, I will stop falling into the trap of Traitors.

83

THE CONVERSATION BETWEEN A MOTHER FLOWER AND A BABY FLOWER

Today, evening, when I went to the rooftop, suddenly I overheard some valuable talk between mother and baby from my inside. Mother flower was scolding her baby flower to sit down to study. But the baby flower was arguing with her mother flower not to read the book right now.

After that, the mother tried to make her baby understand very politely by saying that, "See my little princess, we are not rich one. Your father has a very limited source of income. But always we try to sacrifice everything only for you, for your study, for your future.

Now, if you don't blossom properly, it would be difficult for you to get a value from all in future. Do you know??

How many flowers are dying in bud?? But we don't want you to face those problems. Most importantly, you are the stick of hope in our lives. Listening to the mother with a great concentration, lastly the baby gave a big smile and hugged her mother.

This is the real way of teaching, whether its flowers or human beings.

The night is not scared, The night is an adventure to me, The night is an emotion to me.

The night is that chapter of my life which reminiscences all the lost memories...

The night is that state of my life which reminds me all the ups and downs I had before...

And now, today night is that merriment which makes me pleased thinking all the success & whatever I have got in my life till now by the "Grace of Almighty"

85

Covid-19

In this global outbreak of Covid-19, "Working from Home" doesn't mean that it is a very luxurious way of working, lying on the bed.

A lot of people think so. But, it's totally a misconception. Those, who are the victims of all these, only they will be able to realise, how much easier or harder it is!!

In online mode, whether it's attending classes for college or working from home for office, too much headaches are there, even there will be no time to take breath, than going to that places physically in offline mode.

So, nobody should make any comment until they face those situations.

86
MY SURPRISE BIRTHDAY GIFT

Nobody talked to me since the morning. Neither my mom nor dad. But, what's the reason? I couldn't find it out by no way, because, in which everything was totally normal in the last day. Anyway, I silently took me breakfast & came out for the office. But the whole day, I was too much depressed thinking about the behaviour of my parents as they didn't do it earlier ever.

So, after finishing my office work, when I came back at home, I noticed my home was completely dark. There was not a little touch of single light. I panicked a bit for some seconds. Then, abruptly, all the lights lit up like the stars and I could listen to the warm wishes "Happy Birthday to Our Little Princess" and they hugged me tightly & kissed on my forehead. Then, while I opened the door of my room, I was just amazed. My entire room was beautifully decorated with lots of different colours of balloons, fairy lights, etc. But one thing which took tears into my eyes, there were infinity of teddy bears that overwhelmed me because they fulfilled my desire what I inculcated always. And, I will showcase that day like a Heaven in my mind forever..

87

A TRIANGLE LOVE STORY OF SKY, RAIN & CLOUD

Rain is the first love of cloud. They love each other unconditionally. On the other hand, sky also loves the rain but he (sky) couldn't propose her (rain) ever.

That's why, today the sky is crying because he sacrificed his love but there is a big smil on his face.

This is called the untold and one-sided love story.

88

Motivatition

Life Greets Me

When I never give up, despite lots of obstacles in front of me,

When I never get tired by fighting continuously with lots of difficulties,

When I have the success, overcoming all the hardships,

My life never demotivates me. It waits me to become a victorious and to see a big smile on my face. My life is a book of inspiration for me.

89

Horror

One day, in a heavy rainy evening, I was alone at home and with a lot of curiosity I was reading a detective story sitting on the sofa.

Suddenly, the electricity had gone and I just turned to my beside table and grabbed my cell phone to turn on the flash light. Thereafter, finding out a candle, I lid up. After that I came back to my sofa and started reading again. But, abruptly, somebody ringed the door bell for 4 to 5 times and I was astonished to think, despite no electricity, how can a bell ring?

I got scared a lot but with little courage, going to the door, I asked, "Who's this?" But nobody answered. Still, the bell was ringing over and again. Being totally shocked, immediately I called my mom and stated the whole incident since, she was not at home and I was curled up in a corner of my room. But, surprisingly, shortly, before she returned, the electricity came back and my mom arrived. I ran and tightly hugged her and she said, look at me, there is nobody. I tried to make her understand a lot but she didn't believe me. Hence, my detective story of book had become my detective story of life though I never believed in any miraculous things. But that horror evening forced me to do that.

90

ALONE IN THE CITY

Just sometimes ago, there was a heavy rain in my city. Now, everywhere is existing a pin-drop silence.

Nobody is walking on the road. The roads are wet and fully empty. Only the street lights are lightening and the reflections are falling on the road.

The leaves are glittering for getting wet. A pleasant air is blowing and I am feeling goosebumps. There is too much dead silence today around me. I realise, If I shout, nobody will listen to me.

But I don't know, why do I feel like a cry?? May be, solitary life or loneliness is unbearable.

91

My Room

Today, my room is very tired. Only because of me.

Are you surprised to hear it?

How a room can be tired? Yes dear! The room also gets tired like a human being.

Would you like to listen to the reason? Let me explain.

Firstly, turning on the lights, I keep up late to study. Secondly, closing all the windows and curtains, I stopped her to see the quarrel between the two Indian mynas.

I stopped her to see the love story of sun and moon. I stopped her to see the game between rain and cloud.

Even I stopped her to get the touch of nature mother. Not only these but also using each and every little object randomly, I made her disorganize. Moreover, changing the direction of the furniture, literally, I barbarously tortured her.

Now, can you imagine how much cruel I am?

I never felt her emotions, her feelings and suffocations.

I never felt her tiredness. I never felt, she needs more sleep. I never gave her the chance to take rest. But suddenly I have realised my fault and my high selfishness and that's why I turned off all the lights of my room. And for all those guilt, I really apologise to you, My Loving Room. I am incomplete without you.

92
AN ADORABLE SPARROW

One morning, after waking up from the sleep, I went to my favourite balcony with a cup of coffee and a story book.

Thereafter the attractive thing which I noticed was a little sweet sparrow flew away and sat down at my balcony.

And, in the same way, every morning, while I would have gone to the balcony, I could see her sitting down and looking at me at a glance. Suddenly, one day, she didn't come and I waited so long hours for her coming.

That was the first time I got upset. But, she didn't come lastly. I was deeply saddened even today. Because I fell in love with that sweet baby bird.

But what happened? Why didn't she come to me? A lot of questions always arise in my mind.

Actually, still today, I tremendously miss you my little angel. I tremendously miss you.

93

Dear

Friends are like all the chapters of a book Before the examination they revise all of them But the funny thing is that,

They remember some of the chapters and forget the rest. How ridiculous!! Isn't it??

This is called the reality of life.

Presently Covid 19 is executing the duty of a policeman.

He is trying to arrest all of us.

But we people have covered our face by mask for escaping from him,

So that, he can't recognize us

Do we know at all?? Why we are doing like this?? Because we all are criminals like our impure universe!!

95

Help

Help always doesn't mean giving money or alms to those people who are poor and distressed, who are in need, etc.

In my sense, help means extending the hands towards all the people along with holding their hands with love, so that, we can change their world with some inspirational or motivational words and share their miseries a little bit standing on their positions.

96

Letters

Education is not only defined by the accumulation of words (A, B, C, D, etc.)

It is mainly defined by the behaviour, the politeness, the way of speaking, respect to others and so on.

And this is the superior identity of a person.

97

Eloquent

If stars could speak, they'd say.

Hey, cheer up!! Be sparkle like me, don't be upset. Open your eyes, go ahead and see how many unexpected things are waiting for you.

Just utilize the opportunities to fulfill your dreams come true.

98

Joy!

Dancing is like a hidden dream in each rhythm and holy sound of the Ghungur and a dedication for every artist. It is that motivational think which is expressed not with the language of the face but with the language of the body.

99

I need more negativity in my life.

Actually, I personally believe that, if I don't get any shock in my life, I will never be able to be strong like a concrete in future. Because, in my vision, negativity is the power of positivity.

100

Revenge

One day we brutally oppressed our nature mother Today she is taking revenge on us for that injustice.

What a simple calculation. Isn't it??

But now we are having trouble to solve this mathematics. This is called the pastime of nature.

101

Examinatition

Suppose life is a question paper of 100 marks. The duration of time is 3 hours and 50 questions are there.

Each is of 2 marks. But I can challenge myself and everyone, by thinking and thinking the 3 hours will be over. Because the life related questions are questionable itself in which we ourselves get confused to take the decisions in nay phase i.e.

What is right or what is wrong?

What should we do or what shouldn't we do?

How should we solve the problem or how shouldn't we solve the problem?

So, it's too difficult to solve that question paper and those 50 questions which have no answers.

102

A SIMPLE MIS-UNDERSTANDING

There was only 10 minutes late to come her. She literally ran to met him.

While she came, there was no smile on his face. He was too much Bass. She asked him several times, "What happened'?

But his eyes were red like blood in anger that time. She was fearful. Still, she tried lots and lots to made him understand that she got stuck into traffic jam.

But, he didn't trust her. He humiliated her abundantly using a lot of bad words. Yet, she was voiceless and the water was falling from her eyes. In that way, by speaking & speaking, he crossed his limit.

Because, lastly, he mentioned her as a whore which made her wake up & she couldn't silent anymore.

Then, she replied: wait. What are you talking about? Are you in your sense?

For so long time, you have been telling yourself but I uttered not a single word.

But, now, you are out of your border.

You talked about my chastity. Could you feel? How much hurt is this!!

Whenever someone talks about... If you knew...

Okay. Let it pass.

I am just leaving right now & don't ever try to contact with me. And, if you have anything to say, you can, because, I know, how I am!! I don't have to learn from anyone.

103

THE DAYS LEFT BEHIND

Last night, I was listening to my mom's childhood story. The story about her village that she left behind long years back. Honestly, even if I write page after page, it won't be over. Billions & billions memories are there and that will never fade.

Together picnic, cooking in the clay oven, different smell of smoke of that oven, fishing together, picking mangoes together during storms. Taking heat of fire together in the winter time. Besides, how many games in the afternoon like cooking bowls, danguli, kanamachi, more and more.

I might never have seen those days but after hearing I was overwhelmed and I wanted to rush back. Now, our lives are trapped in the brick, wood and stone in the busy city. Different advanced technology has made people so modernized that people can't even think about the village days. In this era, everyone is busy competing to show everyone.

All is lost from the people. The development of the human mind has stopped. We all have become machines. It will remain a big regret in my life that I will never be able to go back there. Actually, all dream might not come true.

But, I would like to sing a song of Rabi Thakur - Gram Chara Oi Ranga Matir Poth, Amar Mon Vulay Re.

104

THE GIFT OF THE RAIN

Just a few days later the wedding of the Rain. The Sky and the Rain are each other's best friends. On that occasion, she had the invitation of lunch at Akash's house. Though, listening to the news of marriage of his own "Loving Person" , Akash's chest was bursting out with pain, because he will never be able to tell her , still , he always wanted the Rain to be happy. That's why, suppressing his all sorrows, today, he enjoyed a lot with his best friend. Because he knew, that would be the last "Chit- Chat" of them. Anyway.....Nothing to say more......On the way back, Rain gave a gift to Akash and asked him to open that after she left. As per her instruction, when he opened the gift, he became just speechless. Actually, receiving the gift in "The Name of that Person" he loves, Sky looked differently gorgeous & Colorful. Even, seeing that the "Form" of the Sky, I myself fell in love with him.

Hence, it is proved that:

Not only, people look beautiful when "Love is fulfilled", rather, sometimes, "Unrequited Love" is also very sacred.

And, in my opinion, that gift will be the "Auspicious Gift" for him from the Rain forever-
"RAINBOW"

105
REALITY

Life is an experiment like Cooking and its spices are happiness, sorrow, smile, crying, ups and downs, shocks, good memories, bad memories, success, failure and all. Just all the ingredients mix well together properly and then start cooking. Oh sorry!! Forgot to say one thing that if you want, you can mix more and I Challenge, the taste will be much more "Delicious and Yummy" than the costly foods from our So-called restaurants.

106

THE DIPLOMACY OF THE NATURE

It's Rainy season but I feel like Autumn right now. Actually my 'Nature Mother'is totally behaving differently. I don't know "Why"?? But if someone asks me "how"? I will be able to answer that. Presently, She is acting like an "Equilateral Triangle" in which in its one arm Sunshine, in the next arm Cloud and in another arm Rain. It seems like truly a game of Light and Shadow is going on. Ahaa!! Such a stunning beauty it is!! And I am bound to say that this Glory of My Mother is not letting me to move my eyes away from her.

107

THE HOME OF THE CLOUDS

In my childhood as I saw, after handling & finishing all the works of the office, my father used to return at home. A tiredness, an exhaustion would have been appeared on his face which used to hurt me a lot. Similarly, today, I found the same staring at the Sky continuously. The Clouds are also returning to their home after executing their tasks. They are the subordinates of their BOSS (Sky) and their duty is to protect "him". And I noticed that they are very fatigue, frazzle as well just like my father. Hence, one simple calculation is proved from here ,i.e.

Both our lives are same. There is no huge difference at all but only the little difference is of "Hell & Heaven".

QUOTATIONS

❦❦❦

Life will be colourful
if you can feel the flavour of colour.

—T A N V I

❦❦❦

The power of smile is more powerful
than the power of medicine that can heal all the
diseases.

—T A N V I

❦❦❦

Kindness is like homemade food,
If you have it your mental health will be improved.

—T A N V I

❦❦❦

Failure is really very important in life, Otherwise we will
not get to know the flavour of success.

—T A N V I

❦❦❦

Each day is like an each wave of the sea.
Just as a wave stops at the Estuary and never returns.
So, a day goes by and never come back.

—T A N V I

❦❦❦

Life is like a bottle.

All the happiness, sorrow, laughter, tear, struggle,
success are confined in it.

—T A N V I

ᗽᗽᗽ

No one is alone because god resides in each of us and he
has given everyone the divine power to win their own life.

—T A N V I

ᗽᗽᗽ

Never be jealous of other's success.
Rather, persevere in yourself and build that
competence, So that, you too can succeed in your life one
day.

—T A N V I

ᗽᗽᗽ

In my philosophy, Promise is a conterminal of trust.
When a promise breaks, The trust also goes away, And
once the trust is lost,
It's too hard to acquire again.

—T A N V I

ᗽᗽᗽ

On one hand, a dream is a wish Again, on the other hand,
A wish is a dream
So, while you both have together I challenge
Nobody can stop you to complete the Mission of that
Game.

—T A N V I

ᗽᗽᗽ

Hope is a ray of light or a weapon for living a strong motivational life.

—T A N V I

❧❧❧

My heart often searches for a long walk along with the stormy wind in the middle of the night alone.

—T A N V I

❧❧❧

To seek true friendship,
I don't have to go anywhere.
I will find it in my heavenly home.
Because, in my opinion, none can be a true friend more than my parents.

—T A N V I

❧❧❧

If you share your problems to get relief with a problematic person,
Then, the mathematics will never be over.
You have to keep calculating in your whole life.

—T A N V I

❧❧❧

Satisfaction is seeing the smile on my parents' face till the last breath of my life.

—T A N V I

❧❧❧

Childhood is a Lost Chapter of that old book in my life.

—T A N V I

❧❧❧

The world appreciates me when,
I have those qualities that can make people impress

—T A N V I

ᐺᐺᐺ

I don't allow myself to Cross my limit ever Because I
firmly believe in one thing that...
Nothing excessive is good for health.

—T A N V I

ᐺᐺᐺ

One thing I appreciate about myself is honesty.
Because I am not like Dual Sim Card that one in the
front & another in the back.

—T A N V I

ᐺᐺᐺ

Smartphone is that destroying thing which has made the
whole mankind restless.

—T A N V I

ᐺᐺᐺ

The weather has a great impact on the mind.
This line will only come true If you observe the nature
deeply.

—T A N V I

ᐺᐺᐺ

People are variable. They change at different times at
different points

—T A N V I

ÞÞÞ

Sometimes we have to face the situation despite thousands
of hardships.

—TANVI

ÞÞÞ

Situations are like our teachers.
All the lessons which we acquire from the situations
are genuinely
valuable, beneficial and implementable for the
upliftment of mankind.

—TANVI

ÞÞÞ

Life without goals is like A deep sea
Neither there is any starting point nor any edge...

—TANVI

ÞÞÞ

The saddest word in English language is death Because
once our loved ones die,
We never get him/her back in our lives.

—TANVI

ÞÞÞ

Stepping out to the wrong path is too easy...
But getting back to the right path is just as difficult as a
bird can't fly in the sky without wings...

—TANVI

ÞÞÞ

If the sun forgets to rise one day, The whole function of the
world will be stopped forever just as
If there is no heart, the
Human body will undergo into eternal sleep forever.

—T A N V I

ᑭᑭᑭ

My favourite word in English is Parents because I am
very blessed and fulfilled to have this precious gift from
God.

—T A N V I

ᑭᑭᑭ

We should never regret about our height, Face, skin-tone
and much more because Everyone has some limitations in
their lives.
But embracing all those limitations we have to prove
that, We all are perfect and victorious in our own way of
living.

—T A N V I

ᑭᑭᑭ

My anger is like a feather once blown away, It goes so far
that anybody can't catch it.

—T A N V I

ᑭᑭᑭ

I didn't look back when,
I threw away all the cursed things in the dustbin
getting a new existence.

—T A N V I

ᑭᑭᑭ

I never wait for the future.
Because, I strongly believe that, My present will
definitely be with me to deliver me to the future.
—T A N V I

༖༖༖

Until, you will feel fresh internally, No quantity of costly
makeup
Items can cancel your external frazzle.
—T A N V I

༖༖༖

I am really very grateful to Meditation Because,
It truly evermore helps me to connect myself with my
soul.
And, it's my constant believe.
—T A N V I

༖༖༖

I am brave enough to do and challenge those things that I
have greatSelf-confidence in,
but not enough to do and challenge the reverse things.
—T A N V I

༖༖༖

The secret of getting ahead in my life is Entirely secret
Because, If I unlock it to everybody,
So, the secret will not be secret anymore.
Am I right or not?
—T A N V I

༖༖༖

An attachment should too much be rigid like Dendrite
Glue. No matter, they are our parents or others in this
globe.
Otherwise, don't get attached

—T A N V I

ϸϸϸ

One thing I have learnt from writing is:
Writing is a pulling machine. Once, I start writing, it
will attract me to think and feel about each & everything in
the universe surely and I have got that evidence.

—T A N V I

ϸϸϸ

The heat of repentance is much hotter than fire which has
the power to burn you to ashes gradually.
So, think before you do. And, think before you say.

—T A N V I

ϸϸϸ

If you're ever Angry then shout.
If you're ever Sad then cry.
If you're ever Happy then laugh
But never conserve all these in the mind.
Otherwise it will take a shape of restlessness like the
fountain of the hill.

—T A N V I

ϸϸϸ

I am not writing for getting the "Stardom". I am not
writing for getting the "Fame".
I am not writing for being a "Familiar Face". I am not
writing for getting "the Publication".

I am not writing for getting the "Money".
But the first and foremost reason of my writing is to mitigate my appetite for "Pen and Paper".

—TANVI

ϷϷϷ

Mistakes are like eating overloaded food.
Just as there is an irritation after having those, in the same way mistake hurts the mind as well and makes me feel to do neither.

—TANVI

ϷϷϷ

To me, INVOLVEMENT means planting a tree seed firmly in the soil.

—TANVI

ϷϷϷ

Don't be an "Open Book".
Don't let people read all the pages and allow them to get to know the answers to the questions that have in their minds.Otherwise, they will top in the exam.

—TANVI

ϷϷϷ

Most of the friends are somewhat like "Seasonal Occupation". Just as the farmers get employed in the time of harvesting or plantation, friends also become at the door of others
when they are in need.

—TANVI

ϷϷϷ

Every month comes to an end just as the charge of the
mobile phone runs out very soon.

—T A N V I

Even if you light up your home with thousands and
thousands of chandeliers,
But, if there is no "Light of Education", your home is
nothing less than a dark cave.

—T A N V I

If someone doesn't want to come.
Don't force him.
Just smile and leave.

—T A N V I

A night without "Dreams" seems very Pale and Imperfect
just like the Sky without Stars.

—T A N V I

Your "Absence" reminds me your "Presence". Your
"Presence" reminds me your "Absence".
How much tangled!! Isn't it?

—T A N V I

Never ever be destructed hearing the "Negative
Comments". Rather, you should remember a thing always
that those refusals will help you to be more firm and
dynamic for going forward in your life.